GET YOUR INBOX DOWN TO ZERO

GRAHAM ALLCOTT

Published in the UK in 2015 by
Icon Books Ltd, Omnibus Business Centre,
39–41 North Road, London N7 9DP
email: info@iconbooks.com
www.iconbooks.com

Sold in the UK, Europe and Asia
by Faber & Faber Ltd, Bloomsbury House,
74–77 Great Russell Street,
London WC1B 3DA or their agents

Distributed in the UK, Europe and Asia
by TBS Ltd, TBS Distribution Centre, Colchester Road,
Frating Green, Colchester CO7 7DW

Distributed in Australia and New Zealand
by Allen & Unwin Pty Ltd, PO Box 8500,
83 Alexander Street, Crows Nest, NSW 2065

Distributed in South Africa by
Jonathan Ball, Office B4, The District,
41 Sir Lowry Road, Woodstock 7925

Distributed in India by Penguin Books India,
7th Floor, Infinity Tower – C, DLF Cyber City,
Gurgaon 122002, Haryana

Distributed in Canada by
Publishers Group Canada, 76 Stafford Street, Unit 300
Toronto, Ontario M6J 2S1

ISBN: 978-178578-059-2

Typeset by Bernadette McDonagh and Marie Doherty
Cover logo and illustrations by Burrell Design

Printed and bound in the UK by
Clays Ltd, St Ives plc

Managing our attention is the new key to Ninja-level productivity. The reason this is so crucial these days is simple: information overload.

Information overload – not just from email, but from the internet, social networking sites, 24-hour news, work intranets and the sheer speed and volume of modern knowledge work – is a much bigger challenge than it was even two years ago, let alone ten years ago, and this carries a major threat to our productivity. The more information we subject ourselves to, the more likely our attention moves away from the things we really need to focus on.

'One of the most important soft skills you can have is figuring out how to deal with a high volume of email. And the only way to do that is to put some kind of a system in place that's simple and repeatable and is going to allow you to have an actual life outside of email.' – Merlin Mann, 43folders.com and creator of Inbox Zero

Email in particular is a prime offender here. Research carried out by the Universities of Glasgow and Paisley has discovered that one third of email users get stressed by the heavy volume of emails they receive.

When I was a busy Chief Executive, and before I had any need to invest time in thinking about my own productivity (since, as a Chief Executive, I had plenty of people in the organization to be productive on my behalf!), my email management was completely out of control and it stressed me out. I had an inbox with 3,000 emails not yet dealt with – and rising! – and I would all too often need prompting to meet necessary commitments and deadlines. This approach would frequently mean I would miss opportunities to be proactive as well as obviously miss the deadlines concealed way down somewhere in the depths of my inbox.

Of course, even more stressful than knowing you've missed something vital that you needed to act on is *not* knowing that you're missing something vital that you need to act on! The fact that you don't even know what other opportunities or threats lie buried in that stack of emails, and how important that information and those opportunities could potentially be, is at the root of the stress most people feel about their email, and the obligation people feel to be constantly connected to it.

People become a slave to their email account as it piles up even further and it quickly becomes a constant drain on attention. When I was a Chief Executive I was never off my emails: I was constantly distracted by new emails coming in, and spent half my time scrolling up, scrolling down, scrolling up, scrolling down – never actually fixing the mountainous problem in front of me, just regularly reminding myself that the mountain was still there to be climbed. Sound familiar at all?

THE PARADIGM SHIFT: CONNECTIVITY VS. PRODUCTIVITY

Today, my email practice is very different. I have a system in place that gets my inbox to zero several times a day, leaving me clear about what opportunities or threats are lurking, and miraculously, I'm also able to track and follow up on particular emails at the right times so that things don't fall through the cracks and get lost in the back and forth of email. In this chapter I'll show you how this works and by following the exercises in this book, we'll get your email inbox to zero in the next couple of hours if you're up for it.

BEING 'CONNECTED' REQUIRES VERY LITTLE THINKING. DEFINING THE MEANING OF INPUTS REQUIRES A LOT OF THINKING

It's time for you to rethink email. Let's start with the uncomfortable truth about the way that we work. As soon as more than one thing has our attention and we experience information overload, our instinctive reaction is that we want to feel busy in order to feel like we're making progress. Because as a species we're inherently lazy, we gravitate to the easiest way to achieve this illusion of progress.

We check for what's new, we scroll up and down, we fiddle around creating archive folders, we check for other new information (for example on our social media profiles or the news or our phone) and generally begin to develop an addiction to being connected. What we're addicted to here is the illusion of productivity for a minimal payoff of thinking.

Getting your inbox to zero breaks out of this bad habit and changes the way you see email; you instead become addicted to being safe in the knowledge that all of the decision-making and thinking work has been done. The system itself forces Ninja-like decisiveness and discipline that's needed for you to make the difficult decisions about emails as soon as you read them, reducing procrastination time, increasing clarity about your work and vastly reducing the stress that email overload causes.

'What gets measured gets managed.'
– Peter Drucker

The surprising thing – and one that most people never discover – is that once your email inbox is at zero, keeping it there is pretty easy. After all, there's no mountain left to climb, just today's molehill. In fact, one of the nicest things about using such a system is how easy it is to take couple of days out of the office, knowing that when you return you only have that many days' processing to do, because you're starting from a zero position before you leave. Also, your ability to make decisions about each email will be so enhanced that you can go away for a week's annual leave and come back and clear all your emails in a matter of an hour or so. And if you happen to experience a heavy volume of emails for a few days, and start to see your inbox building up again, you can easily measure this and estimate how long it will take to get you back to zero. Email changes from being a task that seems like an amorphous mass of work that will never be finished, into a quantifiable conveyor belt where every single email has a possible decision that can be made about it straight away. Sounds simple doesn't it? Well, the good news is that is really is!

THE MINDSET YOU NEED TO KEEP YOUR INBOX AT ZERO

There are three mindset changes required to implement this system that will wean you off your addiction to being connected to email and encourage you to develop an addiction to decisiveness and productivity instead.

YOUR INBOX IS JUST A PLACE WHERE EMAILS LAND

Your inbox is not your to-do list. I cannot emphasize this enough. Your inbox is not your to-do list. It is nothing more than a holding pen for where new inputs land. We often try to keep emails in our inbox because we don't want to lose them or we want to come back to them. But the really meaningful work goes on outside of the email inbox and using it as your primary to-do list reminder will mean either that things from elsewhere are missed or you end up having to email yourself. A lot. In addition, using your inbox as a to-do list mixes your to-do reminders with all the other noise that your inbox throws at you, so it can be difficult to know what's 'to do' versus 'what's happening' versus what can be ignored.

We need to create new holding pens for these very differently categorized items otherwise we'll keep having to make the decisions about what's actionable and what's not over and over again. Your inbox is to your work what an airport runway is to your holiday. The impact of an email isn't felt in the inbox it lands in; it ends with an action, a reply, something read and filed, or something deleted.

DON'T LET YOUR INBOX NAG YOU ALL DAY

Your inbox is full of potentially exciting information to get distracted with and this information is piling up all the time! 'What if there's something vital in there? Better quickly go and see what it is!' Checking too often can become a deadly disease. Turn off every sound and graphic. That way, you can revisit the inbox when you're ready to, not when the inbox is nagging you to return.

DON'T 'CHECK' YOUR EMAILS, 'PROCESS' YOUR EMAILS

This might sound really simple, but it's one of those subtle changes that's actually profound. Every time you open your inbox, your mindset is not to check what's new, but to make the decisions and create the momentum needed to move those emails to where they need to get to. You can only get it out of your inbox if every option you need has an obvious next step – otherwise your mind will do what it probably does now and say, 'Err, not sure where that goes. I'll come back to that one later'. The system I'm about to show you will mean it's no longer easier to procrastinate than it is to take action – ever again.

REGULAR REVIEW

Making time to follow up, double check, print, clean up and generally do some housekeeping on your email system provides a regular chance to do some routine maintenance and a little bit of strategic-level review. After all, it's important that we measure the effectiveness of any system; one of the key problems with how most people use Outlook or Gmail is that they don't feel there's any way that they can gain control, so they don't think there's anything to measure.

D IS FOR DECISION ...

Here's a liberating thought for you. With every single email that arrives, there are only seven possible things you can do:

- **Delete it**, or file it away
- **Do it now** (if less than a two minute action, automatically do it then and there)
- **Do it later**
- **Decide** it doesn't need an action, but file it for reference or future use
- **Delegate** it for someone else to do
- **Defer the decision** about whether the action needs doing to a later stage (usually by adding to your calendar)
- **Decide** there is no action from you, but that you want to track whether someone else follows through.

Those are the *only* decisions we can make about each and every email. The point is that most people delay making those decisions, to the point that valuable information is lost in and amongst a lot of stuff that should have been deleted long ago.

THE 800–20 RULE!

For a lot of people that I coach to get their inboxes to zero, one of the common themes and questions is about the ratio of actionable versus non-actionable items. Now this will probably shock you: no more than 20% will be actionable. I like to think of this as a version of Pareto's 80–20 rule: about 20% of your emails will add 80% of the possible impact you can have through your use of email. This leaves at least 80% of the emails you receive in the category of low priority, noisy, nice to have or plain useless. I would actually go further than this and say that often when I'm coaching people, the numbers are even more extreme. Email has taken over our working lives, over-communication is valued above silence and thinking things through, and sending an email is often used as a substitution for taking responsibility for practising clear thinking. As a result, so many organizations are crippled by the CC button, the reply all button and some seriously bad habits.

I will regularly have someone with 800 unread or un-dealt with emails in their inbox at the start of a session and a couple of hours later there are only around 20 emails left that require any significant action. So don't think 80–20, think 800–20. For every 800 emails you have, there will be around 20 there that will matter and 780 that can either be deleted, filed or at worst, very quickly replied to in just a few seconds. Instead of feeling burdened by a thousand emails, think of it instead as two-dozen conversations. The stuff that really matters is inherently manageable, but it *does* require some ruthless focus to find it in among the deluge of 'cakes in the kitchen' emails, software notifications, 'reply all's and FYIs.

WHAT'S THE **WORST THING** THAT COULD HAPPEN?

Think of it this way: if your entire email inbox crashed tomorrow, what would you lose? I'm not asking how many emails would you lose, but how many opportunities to get a leg up or prevent a screw up would be missed? How would the world be different? We place such an importance on each and every email but it's the actions and information outside of our inboxes that really matter.

There's a definite nervousness around the way we think about email. In fact, when I coach people, often the word is fear. It's a fear of screwing up, a fear of acting without permission and a fear of being reckless in deleting emails that might later be needed. All of these fears are understandable but they are getting in the way of our ability to be productive, focused, measured and relaxed.

Firstly, emails are almost always retrievable. It might cost your IT department a few quid to go searching through old back-ups, but in effect once an email is written, there's always a way to get it back somehow. It really depends on the relative value of what's in the email versus the actual cost of retrieving it. And therein lies my point. It's not the *email* that is creating value, it's the information, commitments or actions held inside the email. Could the sender resend it? Does anyone else have a copy? Could you get that same information or commitment some other way? Usually, yes.

I hate to demean your sense of status and importance, but those emails probably aren't going to bring down your company, nor are they going to bring about world peace. They're just little bunches of electronic information that we love to get obsessed about and addicted to. They're not pets. You don't win by having the largest and biggest tower of un-dealt with stuff. It's time to get ruthless.

If you're really worried about deleting things, here are two simple things you can do. First of all, change your deleted items folder settings so that it empties not every time you close your mailbox, but maybe once every two weeks or once a month. That way, you've got an automatic safety net. If something didn't seem important to you when you deleted the email and your boss now tells you it is, chances are that two weeks is a decent window to realize and retrieve. Secondly, use filing into reference folders as a substitute for deleting. Don't worry about overloading your reference folders: most people use their folders much less than they think anyway, but with programs like Outlook you can so easily sort by date, subject and sender, or of course perform a search function, that the chances of actually losing stuff in there – even if those folders had a lot more items in – are slim to none.

RETHINKING YOUR EMAIL INBOX

Over the next few pages, I will illustrate some ways to rethink your email inbox, from being potential cause of stress and distraction to a powerful centre for keeping on top of every single information input you encounter. These ideas will vary slightly depending on which email server you use, but the basic theory is always the same.

THE THREE SPACES IN YOUR EMAIL INBOX

One of the main reasons that an email inbox becomes stressful is that your brain is trying to use the inbox itself to perform too many different functions. Typically, your inbox will be:

- Where new emails land

- Where the backlog of old, unread or unprocessed emails is piling up
- Where you're keeping emails you haven't dealt with yet but you know you need to
- Where you're keeping emails you *have* dealt with, as a reminder that someone else needs to do something
- Where you're keeping old emails that contain useful information you might want to come back to
- Where you're keeping emails you've 'flagged' as in need of further work sometime in the future, just as soon as 'work calms down again' (ever noticed it never does, by the way?), or until you've worked out what exactly needs to be done.

So if you're scrolling up and down your inbox looking for some clarity, is it surprising that it's pretty hard to find? Behind any of those emails could be some important piece of information, and even the sight of those emails will leave you wondering what it might be. Working this way, it's natural that your inbox serves more as a trigger of the things you know you don't have time to deal with right now (causing stress) than it does as a productive tool to aid decision-making and positive workflow.

So it's time to separate out what we're using the email inbox for. We're going to separate the inbox into three main spaces:

- **The processing folders** – where 'live' work is kept
- **The reference library** – where old emails we've dealt with are kept in case we need them in future
- **The main inbox space** – where new emails land.

Let's talk about those three spaces in more detail, starting with the processing folders.

INBOX SPACE 1: THE PROCESSING FOLDERS

We need to separate the unnecessary noise landing in our email inbox from the small number of items that have value. To do this, the useful items are instead kept in three processing folders – @Action, @Read and @Waiting – which become our main focus points. (The '@' sign is there because the email provider I use categorizes folders alphabetically, so this keeps them at the top.) These processing folders are where anything you're currently working on will be kept and where the most time and attention is spent. And because they contain nothing other than what we're actually working on, the processing folders actually become your record and measure of your current activity.

Ever wanted to know for sure how many email replies you still have left to do, how much there is to read in a week or how many items you're waiting on your colleagues to complete for you? Well, now you can!

@ACTION

You may be used to using your main inbox space as the main place you look at to focus on your work, pick up next tasks to do and so on. Very quickly, using this system you will shift your attention, making the @Action folder your main hangout. In this one neat little folder is everything you're actually working on – nothing more, nothing less.

What goes in the @Action folder?

- Any email that you've received where you know a reply or other email action is needed and where the action will take longer than two minutes.

What doesn't belong in the @Action folder?

- Any emails where the response is a *non-email* related action (for example, where the email you've received prompts your decision to call someone, look into something, bring up something at a meeting, or generally deal with it in a way where the reminder is better stored on some kind of to-do list rather than in your inbox).

- Any emails that can be replied to or dealt with in less than two minutes – just do those straight away, rather than clogging up your action folder with them!
- Any emails where you 'think there's probably something to do' but haven't decided what the action is – don't be lazy in your thinking. Put it back in the inbox and work out the next step before you continue!

@READ

One of the problems we face with high volumes of email is that so many of the emails that we need to avoid are disguised as useful, exciting and important things to read! If you work in any organization with more than about twenty staff, you'll know that at least one person in your organization is responsible for 'keeping everyone in the loop'. As well as all of that internal communications stuff you receive, you'll be getting a lot of emails from people wanting to grab just a few seconds of your attention to inform you about some kind of new initiative or general update. While much of this is necessary, it comes in the form of interruptions. Furthermore, these are among the most toxic of attention-sapping interruptions because they just *feel* so useful! I regularly come across intelligent, reasonable, senior people in organizations who are gripped with fear and guilt about keeping on top of the barrage of internal memos, briefings and updates that they receive, often left wondering if their bosses are about to test their knowledge and memory of these things at a later date, or worrying about the prospect of looking foolish in a meeting because they've 'missed' something.

The @Read folder therefore provides a vital function. It forces us, during our email processing, to ask the question about whether this is really something we should commit our time to. Yes, it would undoubtedly be useful to read each and every one of these things. But how useful on a scale of one to a hundred? Useful in a 'change the world, light bulb moment' kind of way? Or useful in a, 'Well I feel abreast with corporate issues, well done me' kind of way?

What goes in the @Read folder?

- Anything that you want to scan your eyeballs over at a later stage *rather than read as soon as it lands in your inbox.*

What doesn't belong in the @Read folder?

- Anything where you know there's an action to perform. Make the distinction that the @Action folder is where you keep anything that needs an action, no matter how long those emails are!
- Anything that can be read and then either deleted or filed in less than two minutes (just do those as you go!).

- Any emails you don't know whether you need to read or not – don't move things there until you have made a definite decision of commitment. And be ruthless. Time spent reading someone else's report is time not spent on creating impact and value. So be careful where you plan to put your attention.

The @Read folder gives you the opportunity to save up big piles of reading for quieter periods and periods of inactive attention. Returning once a week to the @Read folder will have you speed reading ruthlessly through things that could easily have proved major distractions when you really needed to focus on other things. So using the @Read folder as a reminder to stay ruthless and focused is a huge Ninja advantage.

@WAITING

Ever been working on something, done your bit, delivered things on time and then been let down by the ineptitude of other people? Yep, me too. The last of our processing folders is designed to ensure this doesn't happen. The @ Waiting folder is where you hold emails that serve as a reminder that you're waiting on someone else to do something. It's like your portfolio of people to nag, prod and annoy. I tend to store up 'waiting' items and then about once a week, I'll spend a few minutes systematically running through each of these in the @Waiting folder, deleting those that I know have been completed in the last few days, and perhaps sending out gentle reminders to those people I'm still waiting on. It's a great way to ensure things don't slip between the cracks.

What goes in the @Waiting folder?

- Any emails where you're waiting on someone else to do something *and* where you are committed to seeing a successful conclusion (if you don't care, why track it anyway?).
- Emails you have sent that you would like to track in this same way.

What doesn't belong in the @Waiting folder?

- Anything where you're not clear on who or what you're waiting on (these need to be thought through properly before you move them in here – @Waiting is *not* a catch-all for the stuff you don't want to think about right now!

INBOX SPACE 2: THE REFERENCE FOLDERS

Below the processing folders, where the magic happens at a frenetic pace, is an altogether more serene world. Your reference folders are like walking into a large public library – quiet, reassuring and full of useful information you might need. It's important to make the distinction here that nothing that sits in any of the folders in your reference library is actually actionable. These are purely folders that you're using to store reference material or useful information that you might need at some point in the future.

Contrary to how most people habitually and naturally manage their folders, it's worth pointing out that the most important consideration with regards to organizing your reference folders is not the issue of making it easy to find stuff again in the future. Thinking in this way leads to one very bad habit that will ruin your productivity.

THE CURSE OF THE SUB FOLDERS AND SUB-SUB FOLDERS

Take a quick glance at the reference folders you have already. At least half of the people I coach have far too many of these. Having too many folders is bad for productivity because it creates unnecessary thinking work just at the point where you're trying to get your inbox back down to zero. It is important to remove any friction to transferring non-actionable items from the inbox, so getting them into trusted folders as quickly and effortlessly as possible is key. Notice I said 'trusted' there, not intricate.

Most people do not trust their Outlook or other program to help them retrieve things and therefore set up lots of folders, each with very specific themes, to try to ensure they trust their folders. However, from within each folder in Outlook, you can arrange the emails there by name, by subject, by date and actually in a whole host of other ways too. Alongside this, there is obviously the separate ability to run a search. Your search can cover your whole inbox. Many people's previous experience with using the search function is that it wasn't very good. True, the 2003 Outlook and versions prior to it didn't have the most powerful search function, but the more recent versions seem to have made this much more effective. And of course, if you're a Gmail user, you have the power of Google search behind this, too!

A LARGE BUCKET OR A DOZEN TINY CUPS?

Not convinced? Think about it this way: imagine you are holding a screwed up piece of paper in your hand and you want to throw it away into the bin, making sure it lands in the bin and doesn't bounce out onto the floor. I am now going to offer you the choice of two different things to aim at. Do you want to be aiming at a huge bucket with a large open mouth, or at a dozen tiny cups on the floor? And while I'm at it, I can't tell you for sure which of those trinkets will be the correct one to aim at. If you're clinging on to the need to keep hundreds of folders and sub-folders, think about how this relates to your email usage. A smaller number of bigger and braver buckets removes friction and helps you make quicker and better decisions. And here's the really counter-intuitive bit: since there are fewer places to look when you do want to retrieve an email, emails are actually *easier* to find, not harder, when you have fewer folders!

SOME USEFUL FOLDERS TO KEEP

The exact folders you need will depend on your role and responsibilities and specifically, on how important the themed or categorized storage of emails is to your role. However, there are a number of folders that over the years I have found very useful. Since I spend a lot of time talking to people about their email folders and categorizations (and can honestly say the topic never bores me despite how geeky that last sentence must sound!) then along the way I have picked up a few good tips from people and also noticed what tends to work well – or not.

CONFIRMATIONS/ 'THE SAFE PLACE'

In this folder I keep all kinds of email confirmations: ticket bookings for theatre events, boarding passes for flights, licence keys for software I've

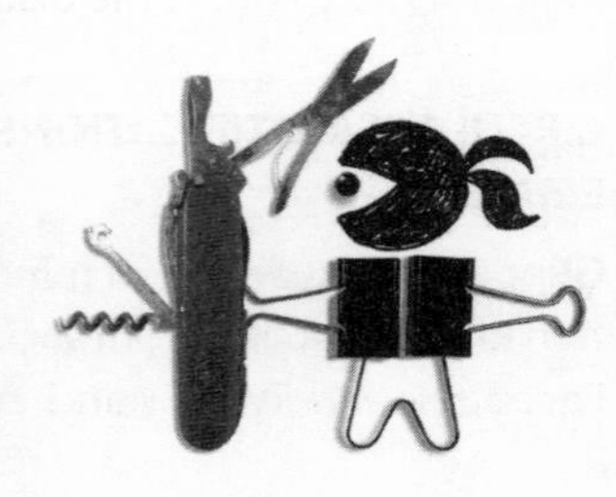

bought, emails confirming passwords or things I might forget and so on.

FINANCE

I store all financial information separately. I decided to do this after spending a day piecing together all my financial transactions for my accountant one year after a financial year end, but it's equally as useful if you're working in a company where you're dealing with purchase orders, invoices and the like.

F&F/PERSONAL

Friends and family. Many people also call this one 'Personal' or 'Home'. There isn't much logic to needing to keep these separate to be honest – it just makes sense to a lot of people. Could I still find the round robin email suggesting travel plans for next month's get together if it was in a big bucket folder called 'Archive' that also contained lots of work emails? Yes of course, but it seems to make psychological sense to put some distance between work and life.

CIRCULARS/NOTIFICATIONS/NEWSLETTERS/BACON EMAIL

Gripped by the deluge of hundreds of internal communication emails, updates from social network sites like Linkedin, Facebook and Twitter and automatic notifications? This folder is a great place to keep all of that low-value noise. Once you have this folder set up, it's time to get Ninja ruthless. Set up rules in your Outlook so that emails that you receive regularly and where you know there won't be any immediate actions needed can be filed straight into the folder rather than even appearing in your inbox at all. You may be asking why you shouldn't unsubscribe from those notifications in the first place? Well, at Think Productive we call these kinds of emails 'Bacon'. It's not quite spam as it's kind of worth having; you don't want it around you every day, but occasionally it provides some real value. Now and then I change my mind over what's bacon and what's spam depending on what I'm working on. At that point I'll unsubscribe from a few things, but given that it's never a huge drain on my attention, it's not an issue that needs too much consideration. There's work to be done, remember!

'THINK PRODUCTIVE' (MINE)/'JOB' OR 'ORGANIZATION' (YOURS)

Yes, I have one folder where I keep *everything* related to Think Productive. One. No subfolders below this. No intricate client-by-client archive, no dated workshop archive. One folder. Do I lose stuff? Rarely. Do I lose stuff less often now with this system than I did when I had hundreds of sub-folders as well? Yes, of course! Hopefully by now, you're convinced of the reason for this. And I challenge you to experiment with your own folders and do the same.

Z_GENERAL REFERENCE/ MISCELLANEOUS/ ANY OTHER STUFF

Anything that doesn't fit any of the above categories goes into a big catch-all bucket called 'General Reference'. I use 'Z_' to make sure this folder appears at the bottom of my list so that it's out of the way. It's usually important to have clear definitions of your folders, but this might be the one exception. However, this folder plays an important role: it prevents you from feeling the need to create lots of folders for new situations. Got that urge to create a new folder for one email? Throw it into 'General Reference' instead!

BIG BUCKETS INSTEAD OF SMALLER CUPS – THE OCCASIONAL CASE AGAINST

Occasionally in a workshop I encounter some serious resistance to the idea of structuring folders as big buckets. Such concerns are of course worth listening to and I've come to the conclusion that there are a small number of exceptions to the 'big bucket folders' rule. One group of people who do like to keep a separate storage of emails in small cups rather than bigger buckets are Human Resources (HR) managers, managing specific cases of performance appraisal, grievance and so on. It is very common for HR managers to keep a separate folder for each ongoing case. The case might include emails from the person under investigation, as well as their line manager, witnesses, lawyers and so on. Subject lines might be quite deliberately nuanced or confidential and it may be necessary in future to present all of the emails relating to that one case to someone making the final decision. But before you get carried away thinking you have hundreds of examples like this that might also be exceptions, ask yourself whether you really need to present the folder to anyone in future, or store it as a specific-issue archive for any kind of official purpose. If the answer is no, the chances are big buckets are still the way to go, much as you might be resisting the idea initially. Don't worry, you'll begin to trust this new structure over the next few days!

INBOX SPACE 3: THE MAIN INBOX SPACE

Remember your inbox? It's that space that you used to spend all your time in! Well, now it performs only one function: it's just the place where new emails land and wait to be organized.

With these processing folders in place, and a good reference library system below this, there is now always something you can do with any single email that comes in. There's never any excuse to leave something in your inbox because you can apply the 'one touch' rule to make sure that once opened, an email is never closed and put back in your inbox pending further procrastination. Ever.

In the first few days of adopting this new, Ninja approach to email, you may be tempted to spend too much of your time back in the inbox itself. And you might also be worried that squirrelling your most vital emails into those top three folders will mean they're out of sight and out of mind. Old habits die hard.

The truth is we resist change and we need to be conscious of our habits in order to change them for the better. So as you adopt these new processes, be very clear in your own mind as to why you are spending time on your email and plan your email time into two very different modes:

1. Organize mode – time spent in your inbox ruthlessly deleting, filing and deciding
2. Do mode – time spent in the processing folders, taking actions, replying to emails, managing your reading and tracking what you're waiting on others to do.

Let's focus here on the time you spend in the inbox itself – in Organize mode – which will see your inbox hurtling from its current position all the way down to zero with amazing speed!

GETTING YOUR INBOX BACK TO ZERO

After any period away from your inbox, you can expect a build-up of unread, un-organized emails. To get this back to zero, you'll need to:

- Hack most of them
- Process the rest, one by one

HACKING: BULK FILING AND BULK DELETING

To keep your inbox at zero, you'll need to be comfortable with using the delete button more regularly, cheating where possible and being ruthless. Remember that at least 80% of your emails do not require any significant action, so you can afford to be pretty cutthroat, but at the same time, you definitely can't afford to be reckless. What we're looking for here is clarity and the Zen-like calm which comes from feeling prepared, up-to-date and in control.

'Hacking' involves looking for opportunities to say no and hit delete, weeding out all that unnecessary noise and quickly identifying the relatively small number of items that do require further attention. Hacking is about finding the cheats, shortcuts and Ninja moves that produce quick wins, speed and momentum. While hacking, the mindset should be ruthless and big-picture focused (resist the temptation while hacking to *ever* read any email all the way through!). Use the inbox views to look for the biggest, quickest and most potent hacks.

On Outlook, the three most obvious views are to sort emails by:

Who they're **FROM**

The email's **SUBJECT**

The email's **DATE**

If you find your momentum is starting to fade, change the view. Other opportunities *will* exist somewhere in that stack of emails, but changing the view makes them easier to spot.

The other view you may find useful is flags. Not everyone uses flags and personally I have to say I'm not a fan (and with this system you can either choose to use flags to add an extra (red) layer of urgency to your processing folders, or simply let the processing folders provide you with all the distinctions and boundaries you need). If you are a flag fan, this view should quickly give you a sense not necessarily of what's actionable, but certainly of what you and others have marked as urgent or important.

WHAT TO HACK AWAY

Here are a few things to look for on each view as you hack:

DATE view

The most obvious quick win. Start at the bottom, and scan upwards. What you'll usually find is that there are one or two emails from a *long* time ago which you might still feel are important, but the chances are, they're reference rather than actionable. File them.

- Email death row. Decide on a date – let's say anything older than six months. Move every email older than this into a folder called 'Email death row'. These emails are waiting to die. They are guilty of distracting you, using up your precious attention, and adding no value. Add a time in your calendar, perhaps six weeks ahead, and if by that date you haven't needed anything in that folder, delete it.

SUBJECT view

- Strings of conversations. Where there's been a frenzied conversation of 20 emails, you can usually delete the first 19, as the final email should contain a string of all the others.
- Subject lines that relate to dates or events that have already passed or been finished.

- Circulars – daily, weekly or monthly round-up emails. Coming across these now might be a good time to set up some rules so that in future these file straight into a reference folder such as the 'Circulars' folder mentioned earlier.

FROM view

- Emails from people who have left your organization.
- Emails from the reception desk exclaiming, 'Cakes in the kitchen' or 'Taxi for someone you've never heard of'.
- Emails from colleagues and friends who send you 'funny' attachments. Just delete them all, they're really not that funny. Oh, OK, save that great one you got from your friend the other week with the kittens. But the rest of them need to go.
- Emails from people whose main interactions with you were on projects that have been finished.

As you hack, you might come across a few emails that you want to add to your processing folders, or quick actionable ones that you can do in less than two minutes. This is fine, but try to resist getting into too much detailed thinking. Hacking should always be focused on quick wins, easy targets, cheats and anything else that can keep momentum going.

Wherever possible, stick to batch filing and batch deleting. You might find it helpful to ruthlessly ignore anyone whose emails might require more complex decision-making and deliberately *not* try hacking emails from your boss, biggest client or other significant stakeholder in your working world. While hacking, your momentum and ruthlessness is key, whereas you'll have an opportunity to move on to a more mindful and slower pace in a few minutes when we look at processing the remaining emails one by one. It's not cheating to leave some of these people well alone until you've finished hacking and are moving into processing.

Once your hacking is done, you're well on the way to a zero inbox. It's different for everyone, but you should find you're left with a significantly lower number of emails ready for processing. As a rough guide, if you started with anywhere near 1,000 or more emails in your inbox, hacking should get you down to somewhere around or below 100. If you started with around 200 emails, hacking should leave you with 50 to process. Those are rough numbers of course, but they are a couple of the common patterns I see when coaching people.

If you're a little bit tired from hacking and finding your active attention on the wane (don't worry, making quick decisions for a long period of time is about the most tiring thing you can do in a knowledge work job!) then take a short break so that you begin processing when you have a good level of attention left for the all-important decision-making.

PROCESSING EMAILS, ONE BY ONE

Now you're left with those emails in the inbox that need a bit more thought and organization. This is where a more considered and careful approach is needed – and where your processing folders really start to prove very useful indeed.

Again, we're looking for momentum here, except this time you're going to focus on each email one by one. Avoid the temptation to cherry pick. It *is* tempting to look for the ones where you know easily what's needed, the ones you feel most strongly about getting done, or the ones from the people you're most keen to connect with.

It's equally tempting to procrastinate and leave emails that might require some extra thinking before you can decide on their destination, or where your reply might make you the bad guy ('We've decided not to go ahead with the project', 'I'm afraid I haven't had time to find what you needed', 'I'm running late on this and am sorry for not keeping you more in the loop').

If you cherry pick the best ones and procrastinate over the worst ones, I guarantee that the following scenario will happen. You will use up all your most proactive attention on hacking and the first part of processing, and just as your attention starts to wane, you'll find yourself staring at thirty or forty of the hardest emails: the ones you were avoiding. And you'll feel worse for it. Getting to zero from here is of course possible, but you'll be wading through treacle to do it.

Processing one by one means exactly that. As you do so, apply the two-minute rule: anything that can be fired off in less than two minutes should be dealt with as you see it, rather than trying to store these in the @Action folder. As you process, some of what you read you'll still want to file as reference or delete, but you should find that as you hit the 'home straight', you'll be more engaged with your three processing folders and a bit less focused on the delete button than you were when you were blissfully hacking a few minutes ago.

THE 30-SECOND EYEBALL

Since processing is about separating the wheat from the chaff, the first question to ask with any email you process is 'Is this information important to me, at all?'. Usually, when faced with that question, a 'yes' or 'no' answer can be established very quickly (remember at this stage, you're only establishing importance, not the need for action!). For all other emails, the answer is 'maybe'. If you answer 'maybe', you need to use the '30-second eyeball'.

You have 30 seconds to establish whether the email is important to you at all. You don't have to complete the reading or replying in that 30 seconds, but in that 30 seconds you do need to change your 'maybe' to a 'yes' or a 'no'. So at the end of the 30-second eyeball, you've either scanned and deleted it, moved it somewhere for further reading or decided that an action is needed.

The 4 Stages of getting your inbox to zero:

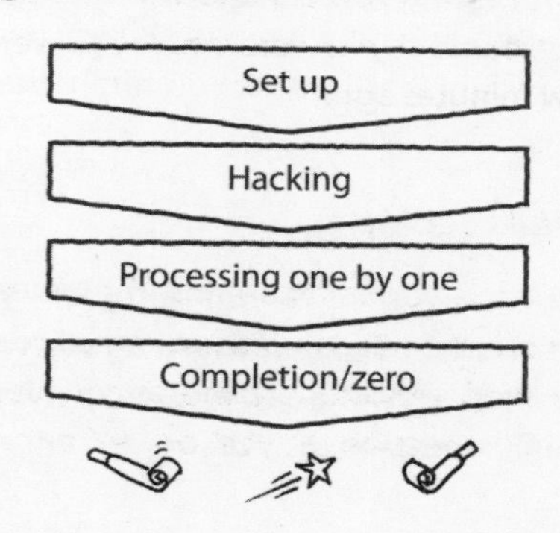

EXERCISE: GETTING YOUR INBOX TO ZERO

What you'll need: Your email inbox, this book, proactive attention – no interruptions!

How long it'll take: 2 hours

Ninja mindset: Ruthlessness

STAGE ONE: SET UP

Set up your three processing folders in your inbox:

@Action

@Read

@Waiting

(Optional) Depending on what you already have set up as your reference folder structure, you might want to make some changes:

- Get rid of *any* subfolders.
- Reduce the number of reference folders you have so that they fit onto one screen, meaning you won't have to scroll up and down Outlook once you're trying to rapidly process emails into these reference folders.

- If you are overwhelmed by your multitude of 'tiny cup' reference folders and want to think about this some more before you make permanent changes, consider using a small number of new, 'big bucket' folders which start with a number (e.g., '1.Circulars', '2.Confirmations', '3.F&F', '4.Job' and whatever else you need). Folders with numbers will sit above the rest of your reference folders, but below the '@' folders you've just set up as your processing folders. This is handy as you can focus your mind solely on these new folders, all in one place and you can use this as a temporary solution while you spend some more time thinking about the best structure for your reference folders going forward. If you're untangling years of complexity here, it's easier to make good decisions about your folders during the hacking stage that's coming up right now, because you'll see when you're hacking which folders are used more regularly and which are likely to be less relevant in the future.

STAGE TWO: HACKING

Remember, hacking is about looking for the quick wins, and most quick wins involve either reference filing or the delete button. Most hacking won't even require you to read the email itself: the subject lines alone in most cases should tell you all you need to know (i.e. that an email is not actionable). Failing this, I recommend opening the reading pane so that you can see with a deft glance what your decision will be, rather than having to click the email open and closed.

Where to start?

If you have a lot of old emails, start with 'Email death row', a single folder where you can safely chuck all of the stuff that's so old that there won't be actions required. This will feel unorthodox and perhaps overly ruthless but don't worry. It's all still there in the 'death row' folder for you to come back and read later, but as time goes on you'll become more comfortable with the idea that you have better things to spend your attention on than old emails that didn't change the world six months ago.

Next, we're going to be using the 'Arrange By' button at the top of your inbox. Click to arrange by 'From'. This will bunch all of your emails together based on who the sender is. Now look for opportunities to 'cull' people!

- Hack based on 'From' (sender)
- Move from A–Z, focusing only on 'quick wins' or until you feel your momentum slipping
- Then hack based on 'Subject' and do the same
- Then move back to 'Date', back to 'Subject', back to 'From'.

Keep things fresh. Keep it moving. Get ruthless.

When you start to find yourself struggling to find *any* opportunities to deal with groups of two or more emails in a single move, your hacking job is done. It's time to move on to processing, one by one.

STAGE THREE: PROCESSING ONE BY ONE

Processing one by one is a more mindful and considered stage than hacking. Make sure you follow the questions and use them as an opportunity to be ruthless, decisive and focused on the potential impact – or not – of each email.

So as you process, you'll start to find that you have:

- A folder with a few emails that you know you need to action
- A folder with a couple of reports to print and read
- A folder containing emails that you're tracking other people's actions on, and can chase them with later.

Don't blur the boundaries

The questions on the email processing diagram here are designed to avoid a blurring of boundaries. It's important that the @Action folder in particular is considered a sacred space and is not clogged up with lots of stuff that should not or need not be there. Some common blurring of the boundaries to avoid are:

- Putting things in the @Read folder because you haven't made an action decision on them – decide if it's actionable first. Only move it to the @Read folder if there's definitely no action.
- Putting the things that can be done in less than two minutes into the @Action folder. It's the easiest way to clog up your @Action folder and procrastinate over those fiddly small jobs. Do the quick stuff straight away!
- Filling the @Waiting folder with things you want to delay a decision about. It should only be in this folder if you've taken an action and you're waiting to 'receive' an action from someone else.

STAGE FOUR: COMPLETION

So that's it! You're staring at some white space on the screen where previously you had a pile of stuff looking distinctly like it was out of control.

There are two types of completion: inbox zero and email at *complete* zero. I try to get to inbox zero every time I shut down Outlook. That for me is at least once a day and can be several times a day, depending on what else I'm doing. As I shut down Outlook, I'm left with a state of clarity: I know the decisions I've made about the meaning and potential impact of every single email in my world. It doesn't mean it's all finished at that point, but I'm totally confident there are no landmines or goldmines lurking undiscovered in there. Nothing is going to blow up or bite me on the backside. It's all in hand.

In the middle of a workday, or the middle of a busy week, processing your inbox to zero gives you a satisfying moment of mental completion, and it also prevents your attention from being spent on worrying, checking or stressing about feeling out of control.

Complete zero – where both your inbox and @Action folder are at zero, and where you have also paid some attention to your @Read and @Waiting folders – is something I try to get to once a week. It doesn't always happen and it's not worth becoming obsessed about (some things do naturally run on longer than the arbitrary point in the week you designate for a complete zero assault – and this is fine), but even when it doesn't quite happen I can get close to it. It takes the feeling of completion to an even greater and more profound level.

Picture it: there's nothing more to do here. **Nothing.**

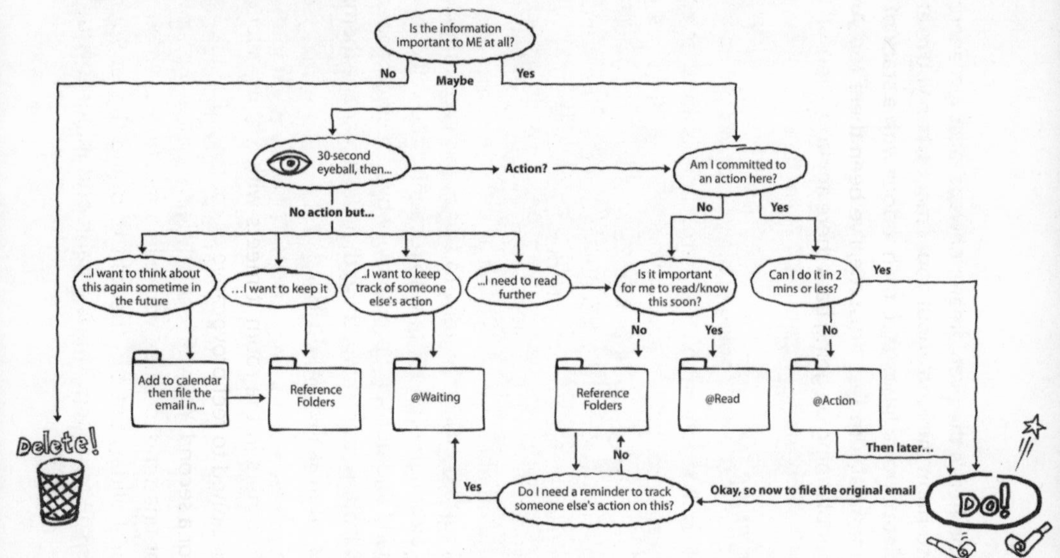
Ninja Email Processing...
Is the information important to ME at all?
No
Maybe
Yes
30-second eyeball, then...
Action?
Am I committed to an action here?
No action but...
No
Yes
...I want to think about this again sometime in the future
...I want to keep it
..I want to keep track of someone else's action
...I need to read further
Is it important for me to read/know this soon?
Can I do it in 2 mins or less?
Yes
No
Yes
No
Add to calendar then file the email in...
Reference Folders
@Waiting
Reference Folders
@Read
@Action
Delete!
Then later...
No
Yes
Do I need a reminder to track someone else's action on this?
Okay, so now to file the original email
Do!

And here's the even greater news. It takes *less* energy and attention thinking about your emails when you're at complete zero or inbox zero than it does with a stack of 2,000 potential surprises. Trust me, I've been there too. And I'm not planning on going back there anytime soon.

TURNING EMAIL OFF

Now that your inbox is at zero, there is another, controversial productivity tool at your disposal. It's the slide on our 'Getting Your Inbox to Zero' workshop that divides opinion like no other. It suggests that every now and then, you might like to sit at your desk, engaged in your creative work, thinking, decisions, administration, conversations and other essential tasks yet at the same time, your email is turned off completely. To some, this is common sense – although even those who recognize the value in 'going dark' and boosting productivity by reducing connectivity will often say it's something they don't manage themselves as often as they would like.

To others in the room it meets with a stony silence. It's designed to feel provocative of course, but think about it for a second. You will regularly leave your email turned off or unattended when you're in a meeting or when you're on holiday, but the thought of doing this at your desk is still terrifying. This is a habit and mindset issue more than being about actual need. Don't get me wrong, if I have a day when my job is to wait to receive the email telling us we're ready to execute on a really important project, I'll be monitoring my email inbox too. But most days, I use the mornings to go dark and deliberately stack up my emails while giving myself some more concentrated proactive attention, unspoilt by interruptions.

If my team need me, I'm on the phone, but I'm grown up enough to know that I'm much less indispensable than I think. You are too, by the way. Your team will be fine without you, as long as they know the rules!

So, if you're like most people these days and you're what I would call a 'connectivity addict' then it's important to challenge yourself and spend some time going dark. It's time for your period of 'email cold turkey'.

Here are four potential schedules for going dark with email. Which could you most easily implement? Which would be fun to experiment with just for a day or perhaps for a week?

- **50–50:** this is my usual approach. I will do an 'emergency scan' just before 9am to check there's nothing urgent, then close email down until 1pm. I start hacking, processing and replying to things from 2pm and leave Outlook on all afternoon.

- **3 regular times:** hack and process to zero three times a day. Early morning, lunch and end of day are three good times here. Allow approximately 45 minutes for each session and then aim to reduce this over time. This is what I do if I am out of the office in meetings or running workshops.

- **The hourly dash:** for those of you in particularly reactive roles or fast-paced work cultures, it's difficult to imagine leaving a client's question pending from 9am until 2pm. But that doesn't mean you can't batch up emails like the rest of us and improve your efficiency. Schedule ten minutes every hour at a set point in each hour to hack and process.

- **Extreme:** Tim Ferriss in *The 4-Hour Work Week* proposes once a week, for an hour. He doesn't even look at his inbox for the rest of the week. He uses a range of interesting outsourcing and automation techniques to make this possible, but it's certainly not something that everyone could do. It's a fascinating idea though and even if you don't feel you could adopt it, it's worth spending a few minutes asking yourself why it's not possible for you. As you explore your reaction to the idea, what does it tell you about your own email habits, or your connectivity addiction? And I wonder if you'll feel differently about it once your inbox is at zero …

- A Ninja takes a ruthless approach to email.
- A Ninja approaches email in an unorthodox way, separating out thinking from doing and the wheat from the chaff.
- A Ninja is weapon-savvy enough to know how to make tools do the work so that they don't have to.

BRING A PRODUCTIVITY NINJA TO YOUR OFFICE!

If you want to boost productivity in your organization, Think Productive runs a full range of in-house workshops to do exactly that. We started in the UK and are now making our way around the world, too:

GETTING YOUR INBOX TO ZERO

A 3-hour tour through Ninja email tips and tricks, complete with at-desk coaching so that participants finish the workshop with their inboxes actually at zero. Short, practical and dazzlingly effective. Also available as a full-day programme with 'Outlook Ninja'.

'Very satisfying. Love the approach!'
– Julia Ewald, eBay

EMAIL ETIQUETTE

Our Email Etiquette workshop focusses on good and bad email practice and teams leave having written an 'email manifesto' to help improve their email culture. Three hours later, watch the emails in your inbox get easier and easier to deal with as a result.

'Email has always annoyed me! This session brought these issues to the forefront of my mind and we were able to deal with them!'
– Nick Matthews, Cardiff University Students' Union.

STRESS LESS, ACHIEVE MORE

On this full-day workshop, we work both in the classroom and at desks to help people implement Think Productive's CORD workflow model, get their 'second brain' systems set up on computer or paper and fill several recycling bins full of old and useless paperwork. Energizing, clarity-inducing and fun, we regularly have people describe the day as 'life-changing'!

'Very impressed. Actually the most productive and enjoyable course I've ever been on.' – Lisa Hutchinson, University of Bristol

MAKING MEETINGS MAGIC

A 3-hour workshop designed to transform the world of meetings! We cover good and bad meeting practices, the 40–20–40 continuum and a range of techniques. Coaching and group work focusses on both the individual and team issues with the aim of reducing the time everyone spends in meetings and making the meetings you do attend, well, magic!

'Really made us think about using our time for meetings more productively and in some cases had us questioning the need for a meeting at all!' – Alison Jenson, British Airways

HOW TO BE A PRODUCTIVITY NINJA

Ideal for conferences or team away days, this 1.5-hour talk is centred around the 9 characteristics of the Productivity Ninja as outlined in Graham's bestselling book – and packed full of tips and tricks. It's also a great way to get a taste for our approach and explore which longer workshops might suit you best.

'Entertaining and packed with useful ideas. Extremely useful and thought-provoking.' – Heath Heatlie, GlaxoSmithKline

HIRE GRAHAM TO SPEAK

Graham delivers a range of keynote talks and workshops on the productivity of work and learning, all around the world. To find out how to book Graham for your event, visit **www.grahamallcott.com** for more information, or drop us an email: **bookgraham@thinkproductive.co.uk**

CONTACT A PRODUCTIVITY NINJA NEAR YOU

think productive

You'll find details of all Think Productive's workshops, webinars and consultancy services on the previous pages and at **www.thinkproductive.com**
Email your nearest Think Productive office:

UK & Ireland –
hello@thinkproductive.co.uk

Australia –
hello@thinkproductive.com.au

Canada –
hello@thinkproductive.ca

Netherlands, Belgium & Luxembourg –
hallo@thinkproductive.nl

United States –
hello@thinkproductiveusa.com